Reading About
THE HUMPBACK WHALE

Carol Greene

Content Consultant:
Dan Wharton, Ph.D., Curator,
New York Zoological Society

Reading Consultant:
Michael P. French, Ph.D.,
Bowling Green State University

ENSLOW PUBLISHERS, INC.

Bloy St. & Ramsey Ave.
Box 777
Hillside, N.J. 07205
U.S.A.

P.O. Box 38
Aldershot
Hants GU12 6BP
U.K.

Library of Congress Cataloging-in-Publication Data
Greene, Carol.
    Reading about the humpback whale / Carol Greene.
      p. cm. — (Friends in danger series)
    Includes index.
    Summary: Describes the physical characteristics and behavior of
the humpback whale and discusses some of the dangers it faces.
    ISBN 0-89490-426-4
    1. Humpback whale—Juvenile literature. 2. Endangered species
—Juvenile literature. [1. Humpback whale. 2. Whales. 3. Rare
animals.] I. Title. II. Series: Greene, Carol. Friends in danger series.
QL737.C424G75 1993
599.5'1—dc 20   92-26805
                                                       CIP
                                                       AC

Printed in the United States of America

10 9 8 7 6 5 4 3 2 1

Photo Credits: ©Herve Collart/Gamma Liaison, p. 20; ©Dave Fleetham/Tom Stack &
Associates, p. 22; ©Jeff Foott/Tom Stack & Associates, p. 16; ©Francois Gohier/Photo
Researchers, Inc., pp. 1, 4, 6, 14, 27; ©Dean Lee/The Wildlife Collection, p. 8; ©Ed
Robinson/Tom Stack & Associates, p. 18; ©Ron Sanford, p. 12; SEF/Art Resource, Storck,
Whale Fishing, Dutch Ships, etc., 17th cent., Prince Henry Museum, Rotterdam, p. 24;
©Andy Young/Photo Researchers, Inc., p. 10.

Cover Photo Credit: © Dean Lee/Wildlife Collection.

Photo Researcher: Grace How

CONTENTS

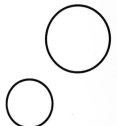

PATCH

Summer sun warms
the dark blue water.
Everything is still.

All at once, a giant
leaps from the ocean,
up, up, 30 feet into the air.

It is Patch,
a humpback whale.
She is as long as three cars.

She weighs as much
as six elephants.

A humpback whale jumps out of the water.

When Patch crashes
back into the water,
spray shoots up
three stories high.

Patch's leap
is called breaching.
No one really knows
why humpbacks breach.
There are still many
mysteries about whales.

A breaching whale sinks back into the ocean.

Now Patch swims slowly
under the water,
like a dark shadow.
Her huge tail
moves her along.

Most humpback whales
are black or gray
with white markings.
People tell them apart
by the markings on
the underside of their flukes,
or tail fins.

Patch has a marking
that looks like a patch.
That's how she got her name.

People who study whales use the markings
on humpbacks to tell them apart.

When Patch needs air,
she swims to the surface.
She breathes through two holes
in the top of her head.
They are called blowholes.

Now Patch is hungry.
She swims under
a school of little fish.
Then she blows bubbles,
lots of bubbles.
She blows bubbles in a circle
around the school.

The bubbles make
a fence around the fish.
Patch opens her mouth
and swims right through.
Into her mouth go the fish.

Humpback whales have two blowholes.

Humpbacks are baleen whales.
Baleen are filters,
like big, stiff brushes,
in the whale's mouth.

Patch squeezes the water
out through her baleen.
Then she swallows the fish
that are left behind.

A group of humpbacks feeds. Inside their
mouths is the baleen they use to trap fish.
It is brown and looks like a brush.

Whales are mammals.
A baby whale, or calf,
drinks milk made
by its mother's body.
Patch did that.
She swam with her mother too.

But now Patch is an adult.
She swims alone
or with other whales
in a group called a pod.

A humpback calf swims with its mother.

When winter comes,
Patch will swim
thousands of miles south.
She will hear male humpbacks
sing strange, wonderful songs.

Why do males
sing these songs?
No one really knows.

But Patch will find a mate.
About a year later,
she will have her own calf.

In the winter the humpback whales must
swim south.

Now, all at once,
Patch breaches again.
Leap! *Crash*!
Why does she do that?
Maybe she is just
glad to be alive.

Humpback whales are known for their very
long flippers.

DANGER!

What can hurt something
as big as a whale?

Sometimes other whales can.
A polar bear can if
the whale gets stuck in ice.

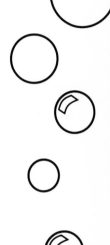

But the humpback's
worst enemy is people.

People have killed this whale.

Sometimes humpbacks get
caught in big fishing nets.
They can't swim up
to breathe and they die.

Sometimes people spill or
dump things into the ocean.
These things can hurt humpbacks.
They need a clean, safe place
to live, just as people do.

Whales depend on clean water.

Once there were over
100,000 humpback whales.
But people killed them
for their oil, bones, and meat.
Humpbacks swim slowly.
They are easy to kill.

At last there were only
about 6,000 humpbacks left.
Then most countries
stopped killing them.
But some still do.

During the 1800s, many of the whales that
lived off the coast of North America were
killed.

WHAT YOU CAN DO

1. Learn more about whales.
   Read books and watch
   nature shows.
   See if your library has
   a tape of humpbacks singing.

2. Don't dump trash in the water.
   Put all trash where it belongs.

3. See if your family can
   join a group that works
   for whales and cleaner oceans.
   Your librarian can help you
   find names of these groups.

4. Adopt a humpback.
   Groups that study whales
   will let you do this for a fee.
   A whale makes a great gift!

People on a whale watch.

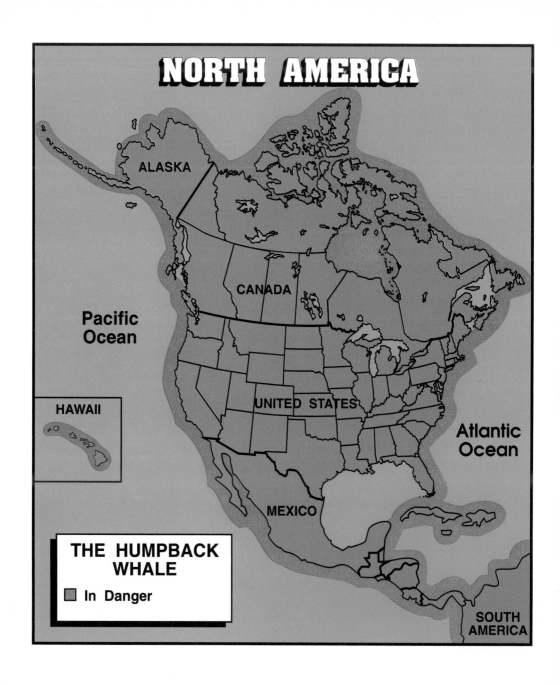

NORTH AMERICA

ALASKA

CANADA

Pacific
Ocean

HAWAII

UNITED STATES

Atlantic
Ocean

MEXICO

**THE HUMPBACK
WHALE**

In Danger

SOUTH
AMERICA

MORE FACTS ABOUT THE HUMPBACK WHALE

♦ An average humpback is 45 feet long. It weighs about 40 tons. Its tail flukes can be 12 feet across. Its flippers can be 15 feet long.

♦ A female has a calf about every two years. The newborn calf is as big as a car. It stays with its mother a year or more.

29

- Humpback whales eat small fish, krill (tiny shrimplike creatures), and other small sea creatures. They do most of their eating in winter.

- Humpbacks can live 70 years or more.

- There are four big groups of humpbacks in the world.

WORDS TO LEARN

baleen—Tough, brush-like filters in a humpback whale's mouth.

blowholes—Two holes in the top of the humpback's head.

breaching—Leaping out of the water high into the air.

calf—A baby whale.

flipper—Long, wing-like body parts towards the front of a humpback.

flukes—The two parts of a whale's tail.

humpback whale—A heavy whale with a thick body and very long flippers. Its Latin name is *Megaptera novaeangliae*.

krill—Tiny sea creatures that look like shrimp.

mammal—An animal that feeds its young with milk made by the mother's body; it has some hair or fur.

pod—A group of whales.

INDEX